# The War against Socialism

# The War against Socialism

*Thom Lord*

iUniverse, Inc.
New York  Lincoln  Shanghai

# The War against Socialism

iUniverse books may be ordered through booksellers or by contacting:

iUniverse
2021 Pine Lake Road, Suite 100
Lincoln, NE 68512
www.iuniverse.com
1-800-Authors (1-800-288-4677)

ISBN: 978-0-595-44148-8 (pbk)
ISBN: 978-0-595-88472-8 (ebk)

Printed in the United States of America

To my wife, Louise, the best thing to happen to me in my life.

# Contents

INTRODUCTION . . . . . . . . . . . . . . . . . . . . . . . . . . . . . . . 1

CHAPTER 1    SOCIALISM: AN EVIL CONCEPT . . . . . . . . . . . 3

CHAPTER 2    CAPITALISM: THE SOURCE OF WEALTH . . . . . 6

CHAPTER 3    THE DEMOCRATIC PARTY: THE PARTY OF
             SOCIALISM AND CORRUPTION . . . . . . . . . . . . 8

CHAPTER 4    THE CONSTITUTION & JUDGES: THE
             LAW OF THE LAND . . . . . . . . . . . . . . . . . . . . . 10

CHAPTER 5    THE PRESS: PROPAGANDA ARM FOR THE
             DEMOCRATIC PARTY . . . . . . . . . . . . . . . . . . . 14

CHAPTER 6    ILLEGAL ALIENS: THE BIGGEST THREAT
             TO AMERICA . . . . . . . . . . . . . . . . . . . . . . . . . 16

CHAPTER 7    THE EXECUTIVE: ABANDONMENT OF
             CONSERVATIVE PRINCIPLES. . . . . . . . . . . . . . 19

CHAPTER 8    THE LEGISLATURE: SEIZING ADDITIONAL
             POWER . . . . . . . . . . . . . . . . . . . . . . . . . . . . . 22

CHAPTER 9    INTERNATIONAL TRADE: DESTRUCTION
             OF THE INDUSTRIAL SECTOR . . . . . . . . . . . . 25

CHAPTER 10   JUNK SCIENCE: WE DON'T KNOW . . . . . . . . 27

CHAPTER 11   HEALTHCARE AND WELFARE: LOOKING
             FOR A FREE LUNCH. . . . . . . . . . . . . . . . . . . . 30

CHAPTER 12   THE WAR AGAINST ISLAMIC FASCISTS. . . . . . 32

**CHAPTER 13**    CONSERVATISM: THE SOUL OF
AMERICA.................................. 34

**CHAPTER 14**    UNIONS: THE WORKERS PARADISE........ 38

**CHAPTER 15**    WHAT CAN BE DONE?.................... 40

ABOUT THE AUTHOR................................. 45

# *INTRODUCTION*

o o o o o o o o o o o o o o o o o o o o o o o o o o o o o o o o o

At the conclusion of the Constitutional Convention, Benjamin
Franklin was asked, "What have you wrought?"
He answered, "… a republic, if you can keep it."

My country is in danger! It is being invaded by an organized group of socialists
(and communists) that want to destroy this great nation, and turn it into the
Socialist States of America. This invasion is not from any foreign land, but from
within the country. Many of these anti-American socialists are leaders in our government.

Recently, it came to me that I needed to do something for my country before
it is destroyed, and nothing is left for the next generation. I decided to **Sound the
Alarm** with a treatise on the current danger of socialism within our nation. I have
no doubt we are in the middle of combat as I write. Over two hundred years ago,
Thomas Paine wrote "Common Sense" to document Patriot thought on the
American Revolution. My treatise, from a non-academician, is a similar effort
without any arrogance to this great Patriot.

It is also my belief that the majority of problems in the United States today are
the result of the evil concept of socialism. No matter where you look, socialism in
America affects our daily lives. Taxes are raised at the state and local level to pay
for a new social program or to pay for the welfare benefits for illegal aliens. The
state and local government dictate where you can smoke and what you can eat.
Judges in New Jersey give marriage benefits to homosexuals without regard to the
citizens. The mass media broadcast socialist propaganda on a daily basis. The
crime in our nation constantly gets worse because the federal government refuses
to enforce the nation's immigration laws. Our borders are left wide open for the
free flow of drugs into the United States, and on and on. Socialism in America is
stealing our freedom on daily basis.

My effort in this writing is to show the Who, What, Why, and How in this
War against Socialism. If you notice, I frequently use quotations from learned
and/or famous people. What a great way to make a point. To keep my thoughts

from wandering and with a desire to be somewhat comprehensive, I have attempted to address and organize by chapter many of the political issues of the day.

# 1

# SOCIALISM: AN EVIL CONCEPT

o o o o o o o o o o o o o o o o o o o o o o o o o o o o o o o o
"All socialism involves slavery."

*—Herbert Spencer*

Socialism, from the Webster's dictionary I am reading, is defined as: any of various economic and political theories advocating collective or governmental ownership and administration of the means of production and distribution of goods. This is but one of the many definitions for socialism. To me, socialism means governmental control of the economy and of the people, in essence, slavery. But, the definition I like best comes from an anonymous Russian citizen in the Soviet Union: "the government pretends to pay us, and we pretend to work." No wonder they called the USSR the Goldbrick Society. In addition, communism is complete governmental control and ownership—no private property. **Communism is the Epitome of Socialism**. No wonder the socialist in the United States and worldwide were saddened, and they still are. Their role model for socialism collapsed like a house of cards.

The Soviet Union existed for about seventy years before it collapsed. Those of us with a few gray hairs can recall the pictures of life in the USSR. People waited in line most of the day to buy food, clothing, and vodka. The selections were few and of poor quality. The Russians would continually buy wheat from the United States to keep from starving. They never seemed to be able to make enough toilet paper. It was said that the Soviet Union was a third world country with a big army. Yet, this was the role model for socialism.

Ronald Reagan called the Soviet Union the Evil Empire with good reason. The Soviet Union throughout its existence incited conflict around the world to expand communism. In Asia, South America, and Africa the Soviet Union promoted socialism and communism through the barrel of a gun. Thanks to President Reagan's leadership, the Cold War ended with the collapse of the Soviet Union.

Sadly, today most of the nations of the world have socialist political and economic infrastructures. African nations are a basket case, South and Central American nations are enduring continual widespread poverty and civil unrest, Western European Nations have twice the unemployment rate and half the growth rate of the United States, and Asia has widespread poverty. Japan just came out of a recession that lasted longer than ten years. In the 1980's, many thought Japan would dominate the world economy. Studies have been conducted that show socialism is not self sustaining. You would think these nations would learn something from the collapse of the Soviet Union.

Let's look at some of the characteristics of socialism. The worst, as I see it, is Redistribution of Wealth. Karl Marx said: "From each according to his abilities, and to each according to his needs." That means, the government will decide who gets the fruits of your labor. There is nothing more evil or disgusting. Redistribution of Wealth also leads to low productivity and poor quality of products produced. There is no incentive when the fruits of your labor are given to another. Mexico is a good example of a socialist state without incentive. Perhaps 50% of Mexicans live in poverty. Of course, the Mexican government is trying to export their poverty to the United States. Another characteristic is Big Government to control most of the activities of the economy and of the people. Of course, you need High Taxes to pay for that Big Government. Also, God, morality and religion are eliminated or controlled in a socialist state. That is because the state controls all and determines what is moral and immoral, the state is god. One last characteristic should be considered, not of socialism but of the socialist. The number one concern of a socialist is socialism. Socialism has a higher priority over The Troops, The Nation, Patriotism, and Religion. This characteristic is obvious when listening to a socialist speak. A good example is John Kerry's statement saying that our troops are terrorizing Iraqi citizens in the middle of the night.

Socialism has been the evil scourge of the twentieth century. In 1917, socialism, dominated by the Communist Party, was introduced into Russia. Many millions were murdered and imprisoned to dominate the population—a slave state was created. Stalin was probably one of the biggest mass murders in world history. President Roosevelt introduced socialism into the United States in the

1930's with massive government programs. The Congress and the courts challenged his power before he could create a socialist state. However, he did manage to make the federal government the largest employer in the nation. In Germany during the 1930's, Hitler created the National Socialist Party (NAZI) with himself as dictator. This was the start of World War II and the death of approximately fifty million people before it ended. Similar socialist dictatorships were created in Italy and Spain. After World War II, the Chinese Communist took control and created another socialist state dominated by the Communist Party. That's one quarter of the world population under a socialist dictatorship. Similar socialist states were created in North Korea and Cuba. The withdrawal of funding for Vietnam by the United States in the 1970's was the cause of mass genocide. Approximately one million Vietnamese and two million Cambodians were killed. Of course, the press in the United States practically ignored the mass genocide. It was for the advancement of socialism. Need I say more about the evils of socialism?

*"Every Communist must grasp the truth: political power grows out of the barrel of a gun."*

—Mao Tse-Tung

# 2

# *CAPITALISM: THE SOURCE OF WEALTH*

○ ○ ○ ○ ○ ○ ○ ○ ○ ○ ○ ○ ○ ○ ○ ○ ○ ○ ○ ○ ○ ○ ○ ○ ○ ○ ○ ○ ○ ○ ○ ○ ○ ○ ○ ○
"Laissez Faire: Let business go forward, no interference."

*—Marquis D'Argenson*

Two things have made the United States of America the most powerful and wealthy nation on earth: Democracy and Capitalism. The world has many democracies, but few economic systems based upon capitalism. The United States, Switzerland, Hong Kong, and some Eastern European countries have economies based upon capitalism. These countries have strong growing economies. Many nations throughout the world have controlled economies based upon socialism. These socialist economies cannot compete with nations based upon capitalism. Is there a message here?

Ralph Waldo Emerson said "The less government we have, the better." Small government provides freedom in the political infrastructure, and minimum regulation and taxation of businesses and citizens provides fuel for the economy. Sadly, today socialists are rapidly expanding government, especially the federal government.

The government doesn't create jobs, businesses do. This is one of the major benefits of capitalism in the United States and wherever it is allowed to operate freely. **Capitalism has made the United States the Economic Powerhouse of the Twentieth Century,** and the envy of the world. Capitalism has not only created millions of good paying jobs, but also has provided the highest standard of living in the world.

Hong Kong is an excellent example of capitalism. When the British leased the island of Hong Kong from the Chinese, they imposed little regulation on the economy. As a result, Hong Kong became another economic powerhouse of the $20^{th}$ century. Not bad, for an island with no natural resources, basically a barren rock in the ocean. Could such an economic miracle be produced from a controlled socialist system—no way!

In recent history, three Presidents (John Kennedy, Ronald Reagan, and George W. Bush) have cut taxes to stimulate the United States economy. The results have been spectacular, and have fueled the growth in our economy for over forty years. In addition, the tax cuts have increased the federal tax revenues dramatically. The strong economy in the Reagan administration was a major factor in the collapse of the Soviet Union, and an end to the Cold War. With a weak economy under their socialist system, the Soviet Union could not expand their military. This is an important point: a strong economy provides for a strong military.

Western European socialist democracies have twice the unemployment rate and half the growth rate of the United States. In addition, regulations in Europe have killed much of the inventive and entrepreneurial spirit. Again, is there a message here?

Currently, the socialists in the congress (mostly Democrats) are trying to reverse President Bush's tax cuts. This action will slow the economic growth if successful. Here is a battle to fight and win.

John Locke said: "All wealth is the product of labor." This is a major principle of capitalism. Of course, this does not apply to socialism and the creation of the welfare state.

# 3

# *THE DEMOCRATIC PARTY: THE PARTY OF SOCIALISM AND CORRUPTION*

○ ○ ○ ○ ○ ○ ○ ○ ○ ○ ○ ○ ○ ○ ○ ○ ○ ○ ○ ○ ○ ○ ○ ○ ○ ○ ○ ○ ○ ○
"I pledge you, I pledge myself, to a New Deal for the American people."

*—Franklin D. Roosevelt*

The New Deal was socialism. Although a good President in many ways, Franklin Roosevelt brought the evil of socialism to the United States. And, ever since, socialism and problems without solutions have expanded for the nation.

In 1929, the stock market crashed and drove the economy into a deep recession. Within a few years, taxes were raised numerous times and all confidence in the economy was destroyed. The United States and the world were now in The Great Depression.

President Roosevelt tried to stimulate the economy with massive government work programs. The massive government programs were a failure. By 1936, the unemployment rate exceeded 20%, and the federal government was the largest employer in the nation. It took World War II to bring the nation out of The Great Depression. Where President Roosevelt used the government in an effort to stimulate the economy, three subsequent Presidents (John Kennedy, Ronald Reagan, and George W. Bush) used the private sector to do the same. Their tax cuts have fueled the economy for the last forty years.

President Johnson, Carter, and Clinton have expanded socialism the most since President Roosevelt. Their interference in the economy and social structure probably has caused most of the current problems for the nation.

It must be remembered that the goal of socialism is to expand socialism, not to solve problems or look out for the best interest of the American citizen. Socialism is also about deception. Very few people would support or vote for someone who claimed to be a socialist. The Congress of the United States has many anti-American socialist, and the Democratic Party leadership is practically all socialists. The Republican Party also has some anti-American socialists, and they are called RINO's (Republican in Name Only). Senator Arlen Specter is a RINO.

Let us look at corruption in the Democratic Party. By the way, corruption occurs in both major parties. Previously, I stated that the number one concern for a socialist is socialism. That being said, socialism trumps morality, religion, and doing the right thing—the end justifies the means. This is the reason why the Socialist Party does not penalize its' criminals and corrupt leaders. This is the reason why a former Vice President can take illegal campaign money from the communists. This is the reason why a New York Senator can violate campaign finance laws without consequence. This is reason why a congressman from Louisiana puts $90,000 in his freezer. This is the reason why a former President can commit perjury and remain in office. This is the reason why a congressman from Pennsylvania can commit treason. This is the reason why former Presidents go overseas to undermine United States foreign policy. This is the reason why espionage is acceptable behavior in the United States Congress. This is the reason why the majority of the people despise anti-American socialists.

And, what is the major tool of the anti-American socialist? It is the **Lie.** I will cover more on the **Lie** later.

*"I detest that man who hides one thing in the depth of his heart and speaks forth another."*

—Homer.

# 4

# *THE CONSTITUTION &*
# *JUDGES: THE LAW OF THE*
# *LAND*

"… a government of laws, not of men."

—*John Adams*

The Constitution is the supreme law of the land. I have read it several times, and it is straight forward and fairly easy reading, even after two hundred years. However, there are many anti-American socialists who want to destroy this document because it is an obstacle to the Socialist States of America. Hitler abolished the German constitution to launch his dictatorship. These anti-American socialists are trying to do the same thing to the United States Constitution.

The Constitution and our subordinate laws are being bastardized by socialist judges and anti-American organizations like the ACLU (American Civil Liberties Union). The trick in manipulating the Constitution is to call it a "living and breathing document." By doing so, a judge or judges can make any interpretation of the Constitution he wants without going through the Amendment Process. Nice trick! Remember, the final goal is to abolish the Constitution in its' entirety. It gets in the way of socialism (that reminds me of Hitler).

In recent years, the Constitution has been violated many times by socialist judges (sometimes they call them liberal). One of the most grievous is the ruling on abortion. Somehow, I can't seem to find the word abortion or the right to privacy in the Constitution. However, I can find The Tenth Amendment: "The powers not delegated to the United States by the Constitution, nor prohibited by it to the states, are reserved to the states respectively, or to the people." It seems that the Supreme Court does not have jurisdiction. Yet, the Supreme Court has created an abortion law that is responsible for the murder of approximately forty million unborn children.

> *"We hold these truths to be self-evident; that all men are created equal; that they are endowed by their creator with certain unalienable rights; that among these are **Life**, liberty, and the pursuit of happiness."*
>
> —Declaration of Independence

For your edification, I have listed the Bill of Rights. These first ten amendments to the Constitution are the most abused. They were specifically added to the Constitution because The Founders feared the power of big government. Look them over carefully, for these are your rights that the anti-American socialists wants to steal from you.

**Amendment I**—Congress shall make no law respecting an establishment of religion, or prohibiting the free exercise thereof; or abridging the freedom of speech, or of the press; or the right of the people peacefully to assemble, and to petition the government for a redress of grievances.

**Amendment II**—A well regulated militia, being necessary to the security of a free state, the right of the people to keep and bear arms, shall not be infringed.

**Amendment III**—No soldier shall, in time of peace be quartered in any house, without the consent of the owner, nor in time of war, but in a manner to be prescribed by law.

**Amendment IV**—The right of the people to be secure in their persons, houses, papers, and effects, against unreasonable searches and seizures, shall not be violated, and no warrants shall issue, but upon probably cause, supported by oath or affirmation, and particularly describing the place to be searched, and the persons or things to be seized.

**Amendment V**—No person shall be held to answer for a capital, or otherwise infamous crime, unless on a presentment or indictment of a grand jury, except in cases arising in the land or naval forces, or in the militia, when in actual service in time of war or public danger; nor shall any person be subject for the same offense to be twice put in jeopardy of life or limb; nor shall be compelled in any criminal case to be a witness against himself, nor be deprived of life, liberty, or property, without due process of law; nor shall private property be taken for public use, without just compensation.

**Amendment VI**—In all criminal prosecutions, the accused shall enjoy the right to a speedy and public trial, by an impartial jury of the state and district wherein the crime shall have been committed, which district shall have been previously ascertained by law, and to be informed of the nature and cause of the accusation; to be confronted with the witnesses against him; to have compulsory process for obtaining witnesses in his favor, and to have the assistance of counsel for his defense.

**Amendment VII**—In suits at common law, where the value in controversy shall exceed twenty dollars, the right of a trial by jury shall be preserved, and no fact tried by jury, shall be otherwise reexamined in any court of the United States, than according to the rules of common law.

**Amendment VIII**—Excessive bail shall not be required, nor excessive fines imposed, nor cruel and unusual punishments inflicted.

**Amendment IX**—The enumeration in the Constitution, of certain rights, shall not be construed to deny or disparage others retained by the people.

**Amendment X**—The powers not delegated to the United States by the Constitution, nor prohibited by it to the states, are reserved to the states respectively, or to the people.

The Bill of Rights (first 10 amendments to the Constitution) has been bastardized by socialist judges. Some of these interpretations that seem to violate the Constitution are:

1.  McCain/Feingold—restricts freedom of speech before federal elections

2.  Rulings on prayer, Ten Commandments, religion—violation of the freedom of religion

3.  Eminent Domain—private property seized in violation of the fifth amendment

4.  Texas Sodomy Laws—violation of the tenth amendment

As you can see from above, the Supreme Court is out of control. Rather than interpreting the Constitution the way it is written, they are creating laws. The writers of the Constitution intended that only limited powers would be granted to the federal government as enumerated in the Constitution. They were very concerned that the federal government would seize additional powers. It looks like **They Have Seized Additional Powers** in violation of this document. It is time to repeal all laws and rulings that are not in compliance with the Constitution.

The primary reason for the existence of the federal government is national defense. Yet today, very little of the federal budget is spent on the military, the majority of the budget is spent on vast social programs. All these social programs were intended by the Founders to be regulated and to be administered by the state and local governments. I often wondered why this was a good idea? Then it struck me! The Founders wanted their politicians to be physically close to the citizens. In this way it was easy for the citizens to get a hold on their corrupt politicians and run them out of town on a rail.

The question is, what do we do with all these activist judges? The simple answer is Term Limits. It won't be easy, but now is the time for a Constitutional Amendment before a Second American Revolution begins.

> *"The natural progress of things is for liberty to yield and government to gain ground."*
>
> —Thomas Jefferson

# 5

# *THE PRESS: PROPAGANDA ARM FOR THE DEMOCRATIC PARTY*

o o o o o o o o o o o o o o o o o o o o o o o o o o o o o o o o o o o

"The people are the only sure reliance for the preservation of our liberty."

—*Thomas Jefferson*

The press in the United States has been sold to the Democratic Party for the dissemination of propaganda. I believe the propaganda dissemination in this nation exceeds that of NAZI Germany—it's that good. But, you must remember it has been achieved through the excellent support of radical anti-American socialist organizations.

*"The great masses of the people will more easily fall victims to a big lie than to a small one."*

—Adolf Hitler

Television news is practically all socialist propaganda. Fox News has a few programs (Hannity and Colmes, E. D. Hill, Eric Burns) that are worth watching, but the rest are strictly propaganda. I rarely watch television news anymore, and the poor ratings would indicate millions of Americans do not want to view propaganda and lies. The controlled news of the Soviet Union had the same problem with viewers.

One tool, based upon the **Lie,** used extensively and frequently by the mass media is polls compiled by propagandists. When I studied statistics, my instructor provided a caveat: **the answer you get on a poll is dependent upon how you ask the question.** These polls predicted the defeat of George Bush in the 2000 presidential election and the defeat of the Republican Party for a decade. Today, polls are used daily by the mass media for socialist propaganda.

*"The optimist proclaims that we live in the best of all possible worlds; and the pessimist fears this is true."*

—James Branch Cabell

The newspapers are as bad as the television news. I only know of three newspapers that try to report the news accurately—The New York Post, The Washington Times, and The Wall Street Journal. It's nice to read an article, and not have to analyze it for lies. I heard the New York Times is laying people off.

Talk radio is my number one source for news. Rush Limbaugh and Mark Levin are two of my favorite shows. I heard congress is trying to pass a bill to eliminate conservative talk radio. This is another battle to fight and win in The War against Socialism.

The Internet is my second source for accurate news reporting. You just need to be selective, and stay away from the socialist web sites.

Prior to the 2004 Presidential election, there was a conference of journalists from most of the news agencies. Their purpose in this gathering of propagandists was to see what they could do to defeat President Bush in his reelection bid. This sounds like the vast left wing conspiracy, or was that the vast right wing conspiracy Hillary Clinton was talking about?

From the last two major elections, it is obvious that the nation is evenly divided on those that know the issues and those who don't. The way I see it, about 50 percent of the population are smart enough to vote correctly, 20 percent are brain dead socialists, and about 30 percent can be influenced by propaganda.

I do have concerns about the moral quality of some Americans. I am concerned: about people that will vote for a pro-abortion candidate, about people that will vote for an amoral candidate, about people that will vote for a corrupt politician, about people that will vote for politicians that make treasonous statements, about people that will vote for anti-American socialists.

*"The function of wisdom is discriminating between good and evil."*

—Cicero

# 6

# *ILLEGAL ALIENS: THE BIGGEST THREAT TO AMERICA*

o o o o o o o o o o o o o o o o o o o o o o o o o o o o o o o o o o o o o o
"The execution of laws is more important than the making of them."

—*Thomas Jefferson*

President Bush has proposed granting amnesty to approximately 11 million illegal aliens, and he has the support of practically all the socialists in the congress. **This Action Would Destroy The United States.** Nothing else matters if you no longer have a nation. Senator Sessions (R-AL) called the Senate amnesty bill **"treachery."** And, he is right the Senate amnesty bill would be an act of treason. Thankfully, millions of phone calls and Fax's to the President and to the Congress from the American Citizens defeated this treacherous bill in 2006.

*"The condition upon which God has given liberty to man is eternal vigilance."*

—John Philpot Curran

I would estimate that approximately 60 percent of the population and the congress are conservative, and the Senate amnesty bill has infuriated every conservative in the nation.

There are many different estimates of aliens that have entered our country illegally. One puts the number at thirty million already in the country. Another estimate is that within twenty years, as many as one hundred million illegal aliens

16

would be in the United States. That would be a 33 percent increase in the population, and it would bankrupt the nation. Incidentally, there are four to five million aliens waiting to legally become citizens. Another point to consider, the failed amnesty bill during the Reagan administration was for one million workers, three million arrived.

Why do illegal aliens break our laws to enter the country? Basically, they come here to steal from the American taxpayer. A study by the National Academy of Science estimates that each illegal alien costs the American taxpayer $89,000.00 over his/her lifetime.

Why is there support for amnesty by the Congress and the President? There are two reasons. The socialists want more votes to expand socialism. They get an added bonus in destroying the nation. The President and corrupt businesses want cheap labor and a lower wage scale. Although a conservative on some issues, President Bush is basically a global socialist.

What is a profile of an illegal alien? The vast majority of illegal aliens are low skilled and under educated. Our schools already produce millions of low skilled and under educated people each year—they aren't needed. Probably the majority are Other Than Mexican. Many are drug dealers, addicts, criminals, and carriers of diseases. Due to skill requirements and other negative factors, many would never be considered for citizenship.

Whose responsibility is it to enforce the immigration laws? The President is responsible for enforcing the immigration laws of the United States. He has refused to enforce the immigration laws, and has created a crisis within the nation. The President has frequently quoted the "rule of law" in his speeches, but refuses to enforce the immigration laws. The vast majority of American citizens want the borders secured, the immigration laws enforced, and the illegal aliens deported. Because the President refuses to enforce the immigration laws and secure the borders, crime is widespread, and drug dealing is rampant. About 12,000 citizens are killed each year by illegal aliens.

*"Whenever law ends, tyranny begins."*

—John Locke

What is the effect of millions of illegal aliens in the United States? Illegal aliens overload our health care systems, schools, jails, and welfare systems. Also, the crime rate throughout the nation has risen drastically within a few years. I live in a mid-sized community and there are illegal aliens all over town. Most of them are from South America or the Caribbean. The crime and drug dealing in my community is the worst ever. All the financial and environmental costs are paid by the American taxpayer.

# 7

# *THE EXECUTIVE: ABANDONMENT OF CONSERVATIVE PRINCIPLES*

o o o o o o o o o o o o o o o o o o o o o o o o o o o o o o o o o

"By their fruits you shall know them."

*—Bible*

Something sinister is afoot. President Bush's abandonment of conservative principles and lack of conservative leadership was a setback in the 2006 elections, and the source of lost creditability with the America people. By pushing for the illegal alien amnesty bill six months prior to the 2006 elections, President Bush and socialist senators committed political suicide for the Republican Party. The Democrats didn't win the 2006 elections the socialists in the Republican Party gave it away. President Bush has abandoned the rule of law and is still pushing amnesty for illegal aliens, even though the vast majority of the American people want the borders secured and the immigration laws enforced.

The political mailers and e-mails I receive indicate that President Bush is working a Secret Treaty with Mexico and Canada to relinquish the sovereignty of the United States to the North American Union (the union of two socialist and a capitalist nation). This treacherous deed was done without notifying the American people or Congress. Is this secret pact similar to the agreement between Germany and Russia prior to World War II?

President Bush recently called The Minuteman organization "Vigilantes." That is an insult to patriotic Americans that are opposing illegal criminals crossing our borders. It also cast doubt on whether the President is looking out for the best interest of the American citizen.

President Bush's leadership in the War on Terror, stimulating the economy, Second Amendment rights, and judicial appointments has been outstanding. However, he is no conservative.

Signing the McCain/Feingold bill was one of President Bush's socialist fiascoes. This bill restricted freedom of speech prior to federal elections, and is a violation of the Constitution.

Fiscal responsibility also has been a dismal failure for the President Bush and the Congress. Ted Kennedy's Education Bill and the Medicare Prescription Drug Bill were totally irresponsible. These socialist programs are a violation of the Constitution and should be addressed by state and local governments. No wonder, the size of the federal government has increased by 1/3 in six years.

As addressed in a prior chapter, socialism came to the United States under President Franklin Roosevelt. Since that time, the federal government has been seizing powers from the state and local governments. Powers to regulate and administer retirement, health care, welfare, and education have all been seized from state and/or local governments. And, the federal government's interference in these programs has been a financial and administrative disaster every since. It all started with social security under President Roosevelt, and ever since the program has been in financial trouble, taxes have been raised constantly. We are now in another social security crisis. President Johnson's seizure of powers in health care (Medicare) and welfare have created additional crises for the nation. President Carter seized power in education, and the education in this nation has dramatically deteriorated. These power seizures are a violation of the Tenth Amendment to the Constitution.

Taxation in the United States supports redistribution of wealth under the socialist system. This so called progressive system of taxation penalizes those with the initiative to earn more, and rewards those with less initiative. The flat tax would be a fair tax. If you earn more you pay more taxes but at the same rate as everyone else. After the collapse of the Soviet Union, Russia experimented with a progressive tax structure and it was a disaster. The tax structure was changed to a flat tax and the economy is now moving forward. A change in the tax structure is needed, but it will take a strong conservative leader to accomplish this feat.

It is obvious to me that the federal government has become too big and unwieldy to govern. Most of the burden of this untenable situation falls on the shoulders of the President. And, the cause for this big and unwieldy government is seizure of powers in retirement, health care, welfare, and education. These battles should be fought and the decisions made for these social programs at the state and local level. This was the intent under the Constitution.

Since President Bush has abandoned conservative principles, he has lost credibility with the American people. Many wait with anticipation that he will do the right things for the American citizen and the nation.

# 8

# *THE LEGISLATURE: SEIZING ADDITIONAL POWER*

o o o o o o o o o o o o o o o o o o o o o o o o o o o o o o o o o o o o

"Power tends to corrupt and absolute power corrupts absolutely."

*—Lord Acton*

The Congress is on a mission to seize additional powers from the Executive Branch of the government. No longer content to make and repeal (rarely done) laws, they now intervene in foreign policy and military operations, undermine the War on Terror, and give aid and comfort to the enemy-all with the help of the socialist press. They are more brazen now because they feel no one will hold them accountable for their disgusting and unpatriotic conduct. During my lifetime I have never seen so many anti-American socialists in close proximity—they gather in the United States Congress.

Fiscal responsibility also has been a dismal failure for the President Bush and the Congress. Ted Kennedy's Education Bill and the Medicare Prescription Drug Bill were totally irresponsible. These socialist programs are a violation of the Constitution and should be addressed by state and local governments. No wonder, the size of the federal government has increased by 1/3 in six years. This paragraph has been copied from Chapter 7 because it applies equally to the President and the Congress.

*"A billion here and a billion there and pretty soon you're talking big money."*

—Senator Everett Dirksen

NAFTA is a un-Constitutional treaty, but no one seems to mind. The Constitution requires 2/3 vote of the senate to become law. This requirement is ignored through a trick of words. By calling NAFTA an agreement a simple majority was used to bypass the Constitution. The same is true for CAFTA. This is dereliction of duty by all three branches of the government.

The late Senator Barry Goldwater was a leader in the establishment of conservative principles. He once explained some of his political philosophy: when I came to the senate, I came not to make many new laws but to repeal many bad laws. It is time to look at the Barry Goldwater approach to government—repeal all laws that are a hindrance to the nation.

One important point to remember is that socialists in congress will support socialism, not the good of the nation or the American citizen. The socialists in congress will continually expand social programs and then raise taxes. The cycle of tax and spend is continuous until the nation is bankrupt. It is the same cycle at the state and local level. And, the reason for all these un-Constitutional social programs at the federal level is because of the much larger tax base. People at the state and local level will be more frugal with their money with a smaller tax base. With fewer socialists we have a better nation.

*"The people's good is the highest law."*

—Cicero

Corruption is rampant in the congress. The only difference between the parties is the Republicans get rid of their corrupt politicians; Democrats defend their corruption and sometimes give them promotions. See more on corruption in Chapter 3.

I used to believe if you voted for good people, no matter what party, you would get a government that would govern in the best interest of the American citizen (not illegal aliens) and the nation. I no longer believe that. Politicians need a short tenure. The question is, what do we do with all these corrupt politicians? The simple answer is Term Limits. It won't be easy, but now is the time for a Constitutional Amendment before a Second American Revolution begins. After President Roosevelt's four terms, a Constitutional Amendment was ratified to prevent the executive branch from establishing a socialist dictatorship. I must stress that the mass media will ignore corrupt Democratic politicians. This is why it's so hard to get rid of them.

> *"No one becomes depraved all at once."*
>
> —Juvenal

# 9

# *INTERNATIONAL TRADE: DESTRUCTION OF THE INDUSTRIAL SECTOR*

o o o o o o o o o o o o o o o o o o o o o o o o o o o o o o o o
"Peace, commerce, and honest friendship with all nations—
entangling alliances with none."

*—Thomas Jefferson*

So called Free Trade has caused severe injury to our nation in the name of global socialism and the quest for low cost labor. I believe in Fair Trade, but Fair Trade can only be achieved through the United States controlling its' own trade policies in the best interest of the nation. The negative aspects of Free Trade are listed below.

Shrinkage of the Industrial Sector: Many companies and industries have closed or lost business due to United States trade agreements and/or policies. I worked in the manufacture of integrated circuits and electronic components for many years. The integrated circuits division that I worked for no longer has manufacturing facilities in this country. The manufacture of electronic components was moved to Mexico under NAFTA (North American Free Trade Agreement). I would estimate the number of lost jobs at the company to be around 10,000. These were all high paying jobs. One of the major reasons for NAFTA was to lower the number of illegal aliens coming into the country. NAFTA was a complete failure, but it did move thousands of good paying jobs to Mexico.

Loss of Good Paying Jobs: Manufacturing has always produced the highest pay-ing jobs. This industry has been devastated in recent years with millions of jobs moved overseas. With the loss of millions of high paying jobs, the wage scale and standard of living has declined in the United States. In addition, two of our high-est trade deficits are with third world countries—China and Mexico.

Low Productivity and Poor Quality: Many businesses seek to manufacture their products in under developed countries seeking rock bottom labor costs. The products produced are then shipped back to the United States for sale. I was involved in the transfer of products to Mexico. The wage scale at that time was less than $2.00 per hour. Due to the low wages, productivity and quality was lower than identical product manufactured in the United States.

Control of Products Manufactured: Products that would be manufactured in the United States would be controlled by an International Commission (NAFTA, CAFTA, WTO, etc.). This, in essence, would be relinquishing United States Sovereignty to a foreign body.

National Defense: Many industries are critical to the national defense. Some of these industries are steel, aerospace, integrated circuits, computers, shipbuilding, and miscellaneous defense industries. The steel industry in the United States has been devastated. In a major war, we are in trouble.

# 10

# *JUNK SCIENCE: WE DON'T KNOW*

○ ○ ○ ○ ○ ○ ○ ○ ○ ○ ○ ○ ○ ○ ○ ○ ○ ○ ○ ○ ○ ○ ○ ○ ○ ○ ○ ○ ○ ○ ○ ○
"Science without religion is lame; religion without science is blind."

*—Albert Einstein*

## The Theory of Evolution

The reason educational institutions push the theory of evolution is to disprove the existence of God. Under socialism, the state is god; and the state needs to be all knowing. If there is no God, then all things must happen naturally or through natural selection. Wow, that theory really explains the existence of millions of species of plants and animals!

I once debated a recent college graduate with a major in biology, and I was told that evolution was a scientific fact. I challenged this new notion by saying in high school I learned that scientific facts needed to be proved with the use of the Scientific Method, and repeated experiments with consistent results. I said I was not aware of any such experiments using the Scientific Method. In fact, I said, the theory of evolution was more like a philosophy similar to religion. That didn't go over well. I further aggravated the discussion by saying that life is too complex and the theory was much too simplistic. Furthermore, I continued, the bible story of the creation by God seemed to be a much more reasonable theory.

*"What else is nature but God?"*

—Seneca

Einstein's formula for the conservation of energy was a theory until the explosion of the atomic bomb. Then, it became scientific fact. Evidently, today we no longer need to prove scientific fact, only come to a consensus. Consensus does not make scientific fact.

## The Big Bang Theory

This is another theory with the same purpose—disprove the existence of God. I won't go over the theory (I doubt if I can), but basically its' foundation is that everything in the universe happened randomly without any intelligent design. Our vast beautiful universe just happened from a gigantic explosion. I wonder if I blow up a junk yard; eventually, will it turn into another universe? Albert Einstein also had a major problem with the big bang theory. He studied the universe his entire life, and found complete order. He theorized that such order could not happen without the design of a creator. There was a time when science and God worked in a partnership. Man studied the universe, and he was amazed at the beauty. He discovered some of the secrets of the Universe, but for most it was sufficient to say We Don't Know.

*"God does not play dice with the Universe."*

—Albert Einstein

## The Theory of Global Warming

The purpose behind this theory is to destroy the United States economy, and to create more government dependency of the citizens. Big government slows down the economy. We live in the most environmentally conscience and clean country in the world. And yet, global warming regulation is aimed at the United States. Surely, there's a hidden agenda here. Recently, I listened to a presentation on global warming, and I commented that global warming was a very controversial issue. I then asked the presenter if global warming was a fact or a theory—the answer was global warming is a scientific fact. I thought to myself, if global warming is a scientific fact it would not be controversial.

Again, the theory of global warming is just another theory without scientific proof. We have been collecting data on weather and weather cycles for about one hundred years. Too little data collected to even make many assumptions. About the only scientific fact we know about the weather is that it changes. We have difficulty determining what the weather will be two days in the future, let alone predicting the long term effects on climate. The History Channel had a feature program called "The Mini-Ice Age." Around five hundred years ago, the temperature dropped a few degrees below normal. This started the Mini-Ice Age that lasted for several hundred years. And, to this day, no one is quite sure why the climate changed. The Mini-Ice Age had a drastic effect on the crops and generated civil unrest in the northern hemisphere for centuries. Recently, I listened to a scientist, Dr. Roy Spencer on the Rush Limbaugh show explain how climate modeling is used to justify global warming. In essence, Dr. Spencer explained that climate modeling is extremely complex and the results are unreliable.

Not long ago I watched a program on the National Geographic Channel, a scientist on the program explained a theory on why we have Ice Ages and Warming Periods. Evidently, the earth's orbit around the sun changes from circular to elliptical. When the earth is in an elliptical orbit around the sun we are in an Ice Age due to the increased distance from the sun. Currently, the earth is in a circular orbit. This theory makes scientific sense to me.

*"Most of the fundamental ideas of science are essentially simple, and many, as a rule, be expressed in a language comprehensible to everyone."*

—Albert Einstein

# 11

# *HEALTHCARE AND WELFARE: LOOKING FOR A FREE LUNCH*

o o o o o o o o o o o o o o o o o o o o o o o o o o o o o o o o o
"There is no such thing as a free lunch."

*—Anonymous*

Healthcare and welfare of the citizens is a personal responsibility, not a program to be administered by the government. The state and local government (not federal) does have a humanitarian responsibility to provide minimum healthcare and welfare benefits (and maximum job opportunities) to the under privileged. However, the state and local governments also have the responsibility to protect the taxpayer from those people seeking a free lunch. President Johnson and the Congress seized powers from the state and the local government with the Great Society program. Healthcare and welfare programs were created, and expanded the role of the federal government in violation of the Constitution. It has been a financial and administrative disaster ever since-all at the expense of the American taxpayer.

Today, the federal government is trying extremely hard to expand healthcare for the entire population (Hillary Care or National Socialized Medicine), not just for senior citizens. Federal healthcare and welfare programs need to be returned to states as defined under the Constitution. Some states are trying to make it mandatory that businesses pay for the healthcare of their employees. Again, socialism is always about raising taxes and expanding government.

Exorbitant punitive (not compensatory) damage awards for medical mal-practice, and frivolous law suits have driven healthcare costs through the roof. And yet, these two financial maladies of the healthcare system are relatively easy to resolve. A limit on punitive (pain and suffering) damages (perhaps $200,000.00) would solve one problem. And, a review of mal-practice law suits for merit by a commission of experts before a law suit can go to trial would eliminate frivolous medical mal-practice law suits. However, the socialists have created in the United States a multi-billion dollar welfare system for lawyers. No wonder socialism is so well supported by lawyers.

*"The power to tax involves the power to destroy."*

—John Marshall

# 12

# *THE WAR AGAINST ISLAMIC FASCISTS*

○ ○ ○ ○ ○ ○ ○ ○ ○ ○ ○ ○ ○ ○ ○ ○ ○ ○ ○ ○ ○ ○ ○ ○ ○ ○ ○ ○ ○ ○ ○ ○ ○ ○ ○
"Ask not what your country can do for you, ask what you can do for your country."

*—John F. Kennedy*

On September 11, 2001, the War against Islamic Fascists (War on Terror) began. The Islamic fascists were at war with the United States prior to September 11th, but the United States was not at war with Islamic fascists. Although we were attacked many times, and hundreds of Americans were murdered, the United States did not retaliate. This lack of action was the major reason for the massive deaths on September 11th.

What does The War against Islamic Fascists have to do with The War against Socialism? The answer is the Islamic fascists (terrorists) are trying to advance socialist dictatorships, and destroy democratic capitalism. They have the same goal as anti-American socialists. It was no accident that the Twin Towers were targeted (actually twice). The Twin Towers were at the center of the financial capital of the world, and this attack was an attempt to damage the financial heart of American capitalism.

If you notice, the anti-American socialists in congress are the same people who support Islamic fascists. Have you heard any of these socialists in the congress talk about the tragedy of September 11th, say anything negative about Islamic fascists, discuss a winning strategy for The War on Terror, improve our military intelligence, or make laws that will defend the nation? The only thing you will hear from these anti-American socialists in the Congress is attempts to undermine The War on Terror (especially the front in Iraq).

These anti-American socialists and the Islamic fascists are enemies of the United States with a similar purpose. The Democratic leadership in the new Congress is currently trying to undermine our military operations in Iraq with a treasonous resolution to support Islamic fascists. The Democratic leadership in the new Congress is also pushing for a withdrawal (surrender) in Iraq to undermine a victory in The War on Terror. These socialists in Congress have for months attacked the NSA Program to weaken military intelligence (and they may have been successful). Harry Reid said "we killed the Patriot Act", and was proud to show his support for Islamic fascists. Giving aid and comfort to the enemy is defined in the Constitution. With the help of their propagandists in the mass media, these socialists get more brazen everyday, and think nothing of making treasonous statements about the troops and the nation.

*"Patriotism is in political life what faith is in religion."*

—Lord Acton

# 13

# CONSERVATISM: THE SOUL OF AMERICA

"I would remind you that extremism in the defense of liberty is no vice. And let me remind you also that moderation in the pursuit of justice is no virtue!"

*—Barry Goldwater*

Democracy and capitalism have made America the greatest nation on earth, and its' soul has been conservatism. It is only when the states and the nation have strayed from conservative principles and ideals that freedom and justice are jeopardized.

Many times in the past and present, the nation has found itself in bad economic and/or social situations. Thankfully, God has provided conservative leaders to straighten out these messes. During the time of the Robber Barons, no rules existed in American capitalism. Teddy Roosevelt (The Trust Buster) provided rules for fair competition in industry. This was Teddy Roosevelt's greatest achievement, and is probably the reason his likeness is on Mount Rushmore.

President Franklin D. Roosevelt, our first socialist president, created a political and economic mess for the nation. Thank goodness, World War II and conservative leaders in the legislative and judicial branches saved the nation from a socialist dictatorship.

President John F. Kennedy showed conservative leadership in bringing the nation out of an economic slump with tax cuts.

Moving forward in time, Presidents Lyndon Johnson and Jimmy Carter made America a political, social, and economic basket case that almost destroyed the nation. It took the conservative leadership of the Great Ronald Reagan to turn America around.

President Bill Clinton did his part to advance socialism with corruption, moral degeneration, and the weakening of the military. That bring us where are today—combating socialism.

I've often thought about what a conservative is and what does he believe. Conservatism, to me, is a way of life not just an economic principle. Here's what I believe are some conservative principles and ideals:

- A conservative believes in the rule of law. This is in complete opposition to President Bush when he refuses to enforce the immigration laws. Lax enforcement of the nation's immigration laws has created a national crisis with crime, fraud and drugs.

- A conservative believes in a limited role for the federal government. The primary responsibility of the federal government is national defense, not endless social programs.

- A conservative believes in minimal government at the federal, state, and local level. This provides for maximum freedom, and the least interference in the lives of citizens and business.

- A conservative believes that the abortion laws created by the Supreme Court are a violation of the Constitution. Abortion should be regulated by the states as defined in the Constitution.

- A conservative believes in God and morality. A sharp contrast to a socialist that is an atheist and doesn't believe in right or wrong.

- A conservative believes in capitalism, not government control of business and the economy.

- A conservative believes in low taxes, not ever expanding government to dominate the people. Also, a fair tax such as the flat tax is not redistribution of wealth.

- A conservative believes in conservation and protection of the environment using scientific facts, not using junk science and consensus to advance socialism.

- A conservative believes in term limits for legislators and judges—power corrupts.

- A conservative believes in strict interpretation of the Constitution.

- A conservative believes in defending the Second Amendment and the Constitution. It is estimated that there are 2,500,000 incidents each year where firearms are used in self defense. A socialist believes in the destruction of the Constitution.

- A conservative believes in confronting and prosecuting enemies of the nation. A socialist believes in giving rights to the enemies of the nation.

- A conservative believes that the states are responsible for education, healthcare and welfare.

- A conservative believes that healthcare and retirement are personal responsibilities.

- A conservative believes in telling people what he or she stands for. A socialist believes in propaganda to control the people.

- A conservative believes in taking the fight to the enemy—the socialist.

- A conservative is patriotic and supports his country. Contrast this, to members of Congress making treasonous statements at home and abroad.

- A conservative believes as government advances, liberty retreats. And, government can create more problems than solutions.

- A conservative believes in the repeal of unjust and immoral laws.

- A conservative believes that only democracy and capitalism can solve the world's political and economic problems.

- A conservative believes that a socialist is someone looking for a "free lunch."

- A conservative believes that the family is the foundation of society (not government), and society is affected by the health of the family.

- A conservative believes in a few good laws, not many bad laws.

- A conservative believes in friendly relations with reciprocal nations. Socialists believe in the destruction of the United States and the promotion of global socialism.

# 14

## UNIONS: THE WORKERS PARADISE

o o o o o o o o o o o o o o o o o o o o o o o o o o o o o o o o o o
"All animals are equal, but some animals are more equal than others."

—*George Orwell*

In the beginning, unions were established to provide bargaining power for low skilled workers. We have come a long way. Today, one of the largest unions in the country is for government workers—this would make Karl Marx proud. **The Workers Paradise has been established.**

Initially, unions were not allowed for government workers, teachers, police, firefighters, etc. These were all jobs essential to providing continuous and reliable public service for the citizens. All that has changed over the years and our taxes have been raised accordingly to support this new system of social welfare. In many states, there is never enough tax money to pay for these high paid union workers.

I worked with and managed union workers in the manufacturing arena for about twenty years. Union workers in manufacturing were some of the highest paid workers in the nation. Unfortunately, most of these union jobs have been shipped to foreign countries to take advantage of the non-union labor (with minimal social benefits).

In recent years, the number of union workers in the private sector has decreased significantly (less than 20% of the workforce), while the number of union workers in government has expanded. These facts point to an unwanted situation: we have many non-union workers supporting a high paid unionized government workforce. This is an ideal situation for a government dominated society. As I see it, unions should not be supported with taxpayer dollars.

Unions in America have advanced well beyond its initial purpose to give some bargaining power to low skilled workers. We now have unionized ballplayers earning millions in salary. This is totally ridiculous!

Unions in some respects are an ideal socialist organization. Equalizing wages for members regardless of their contribution or individual effort is one of the main goals. Individualism is discouraged, and personal achievements are seldom recognized and rewarded. In addition, one of the worst aspects of unions is the contribution to Democratic political campaigns without the approval of the individual members. This is corruption of the highest order to bypass campaign finance laws to support socialist candidates.

In conclusion, I see three issues with unions that should be rectified: unions should not be funded by taxpayer dollars, unions should be abolished for high skill high pay industries, and unions should have the same limitation in political campaigns as corporations. These actions would reverse much of the damage from socialism.

# 15

## *WHAT CAN BE DONE?*

○ ○ ○ ○ ○ ○ ○ ○ ○ ○ ○ ○ ○ ○ ○ ○ ○ ○ ○ ○ ○ ○ ○ ○ ○ ○ ○ ○ ○ ○ ○ ○ ○ ○

"The only thing necessary for the triumph of evil is for good men to do nothing."

*—Edmund Burke*

A few years ago I was listening to talk radio, and a former Russian citizen called in. He lived in Russia during the Soviet Union era and was talking about the domination of the people in the socialist state. He said "this is what happens when you don't fight the socialists." His comment has stayed with me a long time.

Remember it is your nation to defend, and if the socialists get the chance they will destroy it. Currently, the Democrats control congress (by a slim toe hold) and they are on a two year mission to do as much damage as possible to the political, social, economic, and military infrastructure of the United States. Thomas Jefferson (what a great man!) said: "Every citizen should be a soldier. This was the case with the Greeks and the Romans, and must be that of every free state." If you don't fight for your liberty, the government will take it away.

In the previous chapters we covered the Who, What, and Why of socialism. Now I will attempt to identify the How of socialism—you may have ideas of your own. The main point is to **Fight**. There are many battles ahead.

*"I'm going to fight hard, I'm going to give them hell."*

*—Harry S. Truman*

- I'm writing this treatise to expose the evils of socialism. Hopefully, it will get enough distribution to make a difference. Maybe, an opinion letter to your local newspaper or the New York Post will have a major impact.

- We need to take back control of the Republican Party from the socialists. I financially support conservative candidates I like in the Republican Party. I don't normally support the party directly—my money may go to some socialist cause. The Democratic Party doesn't have any more conservative candidates left. That makes it easy.

- I also help out at party headquarters making phone calls, going door to door, and supporting political rallies for conservative candidates.

- Support organizations that are for border security, enforcement of immigration laws and deportation of illegal aliens. Remember illegal aliens are the biggest socialist threat to the nation.

- Don't watch, read, or listen to political propaganda. You'll be wasting you time sorting out the lies and propaganda. See Chapter 5.

- If a politician does not support the troops (and there are many), don't support him/her, they're not only unpatriotic they're socialists. They're easy to spot: Hillary Clinton, John Kerry, etc.

- Phone calls to talk radio or television to express your opinion are also a good idea. Talk radio shows with Rush Limbaugh, Mark Levin, and Sean Hannity are a good choice. But remember, television news is controlled by the Democratic Party and is mostly propaganda.

- If you get the chance to participate in a rally against socialism or a socialist candidate—Do It. It was once said "a little revolution every now and then is a good thing."

- Don't try to debate a brain dead socialist. It's a lost cause. Thankfully, that's only one in five people you meet. However, quickly depart from that person. They may have some other contagious disease.

- I also support special interest groups that I believe. The Swift Boaters, NRA and Minuteman come to mind. The Swift Boaters did a magnificent job exposing John Kerry. At one time, I used to think if you voted for good politicians they would look out for the best interest of the American citizen—not true. Sometimes you need an outside organization to keep the corrupt politicians at bay.

- Do challenge any political candidate expressing a socialist view by any means available. The challenges are pretty easy since most socialist positions are stupid and they don't make sense.

- If you get the chance, expose a propagandist. They're not hard to spot. They usually tell a lie every two minutes. Remember, a propagandist is there to slant the truth, set the record straight.

- If you get the chance to push for the resignation of a corrupt politician—Do It. If you get the chance to push for the impeachment of a corrupt judge—Do It.

- Join the National Rifle Association (NRA) even if you don't own a gun. They are an excellent defender of the Second Amendment and the Constitution. They also have a number of political rallies where you can participate.

- If you have the time, volunteer for a political candidate you like. Become an activist!

- Support and promote actions and candidates that want to return retirement, welfare, health care and education to the state and local governments.

- Support and promote actions and candidates that want to change our tax structure to a flat tax.

- Support and promote a Constitutional Amendment for term limits for legislators and judges. The nation can't take much more corruption in the government.

- Don't, if you can, support a third party candidate. That's how we got eight years of Bill Clinton.

- Don't financially support an anti-American socialist or an anti-American socialist organization—Hollywood wacko socialists, Democratic Party, socialists in Congress, Miller Brewing Company, ACLU, NAACP, United Nations, NPR, etc.

- Use e-mail to get your opinion out and receive information. I receive a lot of political information from conservative groups via e-mail.

- Most Important—Vote.

*"The ballot is stronger than the bullet."*

—Abraham Lincoln

Good Luck!

○ ○ ○ ○ ○ ○ ○ ○ ○ ○ ○ ○ ○ ○ ○ ○ ○ ○ ○ ○ ○ ○ ○ ○ ○ ○ ○ ○ ○ ○ ○ ○ ○ ○ ○ ○

At the conclusion of the Constitutional Convention, Benjamin Franklin was asked, "What have you wrought?"
He answered, "… a republic, if you can keep it."

A concerned citizen is fed up as he watches the Democratic Party turn into a radical anti-American socialist organization bent on the destruction of his country. Mr. Lord writes: my country is in danger! It is being invaded by an organized group of socialists (and communists) that want to destroy this great nation and turn it into the Socialist States of America. This invasion is not from any foreign land, but from within the country. Many of these anti-American socialists are leaders in our government.

The War against Socialism exposes the menacing threat to America's economic, military, political, and social infrastructure. It is the author's belief that the majority of problems in the United States today are the result of the evil concept of socialism.

# ABOUT THE AUTHOR

Mr. Lord has a degree in Accounting from Oklahoma State University. In addition, he has certifications in Sales, Telecommunications, Computers, and Networking. Over a career that spans 35 years, the author has worked in varied disciplines and fields that include Accounting, Management, Manufacturing, Sales, and Telecommunications. With his free time, he substitute teaches at local area high schools.

He is a fan of amateur wrestling and football. Mr. Lord also enjoys the outdoors and frequently takes to the field for hunting, fishing, and target shooting.

978-0-595-44148-8
0-595-44148-3